Mosaic PICTURE QUILTS

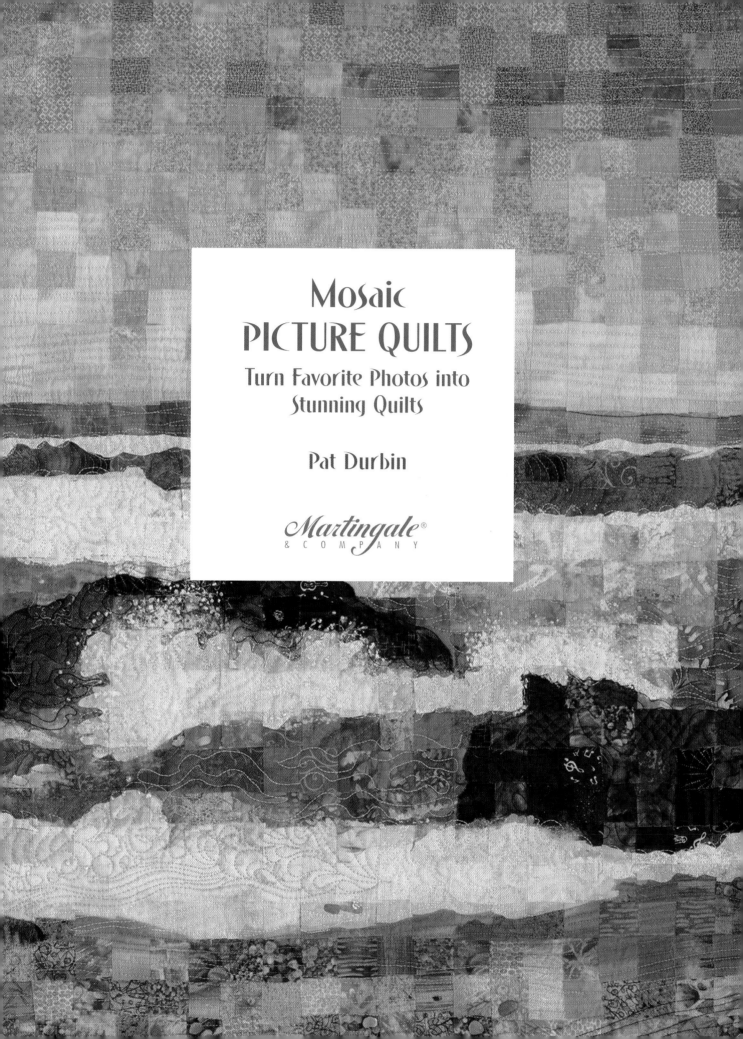

Mosaic
PICTURE QUILTS
Turn Favorite Photos into Stunning Quilts

Pat Durbin

Martingale®
& COMPANY

Mosaic Picture Quilts: Turn Favorite Photos into
Stunning Quilts
© 2007 by Pat Durbin

That Patchwork Place® is an imprint of
Martingale & Company®.

Martingale & Company
20205 144th Ave. NE
Woodinville, WA 98072-8478 USA
www.martingale-pub.com

Printed in China
12 11 10 09 08 07   8 7 6 5 4 3 2 1

Library of Congress Cataloging-in-Publication Data
Library of Congress Control Number: 2007028363

ISBN: 978-1-56477-735-5

CREDITS

President & CEO ∼ Tom Wierzbicki

Publisher ∼ Jane Hamada

Editorial Director ∼ Mary V. Green

Managing Editor ∼ Tina Cook

Developmental Editor ∼ Karen Costello Soltys

Technical Editor ∼ Nancy Mahoney

Copy Editor ∼ Durby Peterson

Design Director ∼ Stan Green

Assistant Design Director ∼ Regina Girard

Illustrator ∼ Adrienne Smitke

Cover & Text Designer ∼ Shelly Garrison

Photographer ∼ Brent Kane

MISSION STATEMENT

Dedicated to providing quality products
and service to inspire creativity.

DEDICATION

This book is dedicated to quilters from beginners to those with experienced hands. May you be inspired to try new things and dream of comfort and beauty through the art you create for your families and friends.

ACKNOWLEDGMENTS

Thanks to God for gifting my life with talents and opportunities. He has enriched me in so many ways. Without Him, I could do nothing.

My thanks to people of the past:

- Grandma Jennie (Bunch) Haines of Oakland, Oregon, and Great-Aunt Ruth (Heberly) Selves of Salina, Kansas. I slept under their beautiful quilts while growing up, and from these women I learned to dream of quilting. They are the family examples who set my standard of what quilting should be. I couldn't live up to their handmade work examples, but I found my own path.

- Mother, Sanna (Haines) Heberly, who encouraged me to sew at a very early age. She let me use her scraps and sewing machine to create with, and she gave me a loving, accepting atmosphere to grow in.

And to those in the present:

- A special thank-you to Brenda Lou Scott, who urges me to stretch, and to LoRen Justice, who is my cheerleader and gives helpful opinions (when I ask).

- The Tuesday group at Scottie Dog Quilts, who dutifully "ooh and aah" at show-and-tell moments. What would we do without the enthusiasm of other quilters?

- My church family at Ridgewood Heights. You've supported me in so many ways.

- The Redwood Empire Quilters Guild members, who teach new and experienced quilters and also do good "quilt" deeds in the community. Keep up the good work.

- My students, eager to learn, willing to try new things, and always encouraging to me.

- Many quilters I don't really know, who have shared their talents and ideas through magazines, TV, and books. I have learned so much from you.

- Then, of course, there's my husband, Gary. He hangs quilts; builds ladders, shelves, and tables; takes pictures; gives advice; and generally encourages me to continue what I love doing. What a guy! I am blessed to have him.

CONTENTS

Introduction ∼ 8   Picture-Quilt Techniques ∼ 11

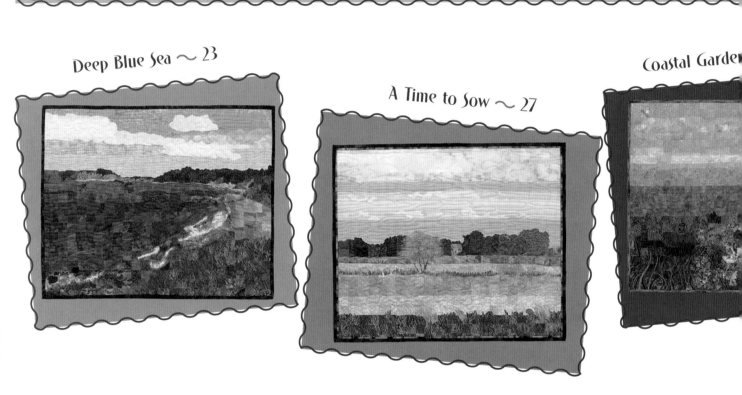

Deep Blue Sea ∼ 23

A Time to Sow ∼ 27

Coastal Garde

Finishing Techniques ∼ 45   Gallery ∼ 52   Photomaps ∼ 56

Transparency Forms ∼ 61   About the Author ∼ 64

∼ 31

Pacific Beach ∼ 37

Morning Light ∼ 41

INTRODUCTION

Agate Beach

In these pages I will share my secrets for creating beautiful pictures with fabric. My new landscape method maintains the patchwork feel that we all love, yet it enables you to depart from the square look and define the many lines and angles that are needed to make your quilt picture look realistic. You will feel as though you are painting a picture with fabric or putting together a jigsaw puzzle (except that you get to make the pieces).

Have you ever wanted to make a quilted wall hanging of a favorite photo? Well, I have too, but I tried several methods and didn't really like the process or the results. So, I came up with an easier way to get the job done, and I like the results. I think you will too.

My first mosaic quilt, "Portrait of a Girl," was done in the traditional manner with sewn seams. I used a pixelated picture for my map, and I used gridded fusible interfacing as a foundation.

This picture features my granddaughter, Amy, when she was 10 years old. When I made it I really liked it, but I didn't like the look of the seams. They're bulky because of the fusible interfacing. This quilt was also rather cumbersome to work with, and before the seams were sewn, the quilt was *huge*! The size makes it harder to see what you're doing as you build the picture. I decided there must be another way.

I'd seen art quilts with an overlay of tulle that held down ribbons and things, and I thought tulle could be used over the raw edges to make a more finished look. Soon my idea was born: I would do a raw-edge mosaic and overlay it with tulle. I didn't want any gaps to show between the pieces, so I thought a ¼" overlap would be enough to keep things nice and tidy, and I would work in the real finished size.

Portrait of a Girl

Close-up of "Agate Beach." At bottom, I placed agates and rocks from the real beach under the tulle.

When you're using a pixelated version of a picture, you're working completely with squares, and this works well with a sewn method. To give myself freedom to shape the elements of the photo, I decided to make my grid a different way. I used a gridded transparency overlay on top of the photo, which allowed me to follow the grid with squares for the patchwork look and also to shape the elements within those squares to get a clean outline of the shapes in the photo. I think this is a happy combination.

My husband is a very good amateur photographer who has taken many photos of the ocean where we live. One of those photos is a real favorite, and I decided to use it for my first attempt at the new, improved piecing technique. It was a complete experiment at this point, and it worked surprisingly well for launching this new method.

This quilt, called "Agate Beach," was my first raw-edge mosaic. The result is a new kind of patchwork look and a very doable method for creating pictures.

After showing the quilt to friends at my local quilt shop, I was encouraged to make a smaller version and teach the method. I have taught several of these classes and the students have very good results with their own quilts. One of the exciting things about teaching a class using this method is that everyone comes with a different fabric selection to use for the different elements. Every person works with the same photo, but different moods emerge with their individual choices of fabric. The finished quilts, although different, all look like the photo that inspired them and all turn out beautifully. I stand amazed!

In this book you will find an overview of the unusual techniques used in my nontraditional piecing method, a selection of projects to make, and helpful techniques for finishing the projects. You will also find suggestions for using your *own* photos to create unique quilts.

The quilts in this book are designed as wall hangings. This method gives you freedom to duplicate the positions and shapes of items in each photo accurately and gives the feeling that you are painting a picture with fabric as your palette. I think it's fun—I hope you'll think so as well.

PICTURE-QUILT TECHNIQUES

It's fun. It's different. It feels like painting. And it's easy! You'll discover that you can make picture quilts that you never thought you could. In this section, I explain the different techniques for making a picture quilt with this new method. The other (more traditional) techniques you will use to finish your quilt are detailed in "Finishing Techniques" on page 45.

What's so different about this method?

- This is a raw-edge patchwork technique, so there is no sewing until the quilting stage.

- The likeness of the photo is enlarged by using a basic grid-enlargement method.

- A gridded fusible foundation temporarily holds the fabric pieces in place. This is a light, fusible interfacing material that has lines on it in grid form.

- Fabric glue is used on pieces that will not touch the fusible interfacing.

- Tulle is a very fine netting that is placed over the quilt picture to hold down all the raw edges.

- Extra embellishments, such as tiny rocks, sticks, and dried or silk flowers, can be added under the tulle before quilting.

Supplies

I am fortunate to have some of my grandmother's quilt-block samples and templates. The templates are cut from cereal boxes, used envelopes, and church bulletins. She made many quilts, stitching them by hand or machine and then hand quilting them. Think how many she could have made with our modern tools.

That was yesterday—this is today. I recommend that you use the following tools.

Rotary cutter and mat. The first time I used a rotary cutter and mat, I thought, Where have these been all my life? The ease with which you can cut and the precision you get are just wonderful. If you don't have a rotary cutter, now's the time to buy one; you won't want to cut hundreds of $1\frac{1}{4}$" squares without it. An 18" x 24" rotary-cutting mat works well for the projects in this book.

Rotary-cutting ruler. I use a 6" x 24" ruler; I also find that a $12\frac{1}{2}$" square ruler is helpful for squaring up the quilt.

Paper-cutting scissors. You'll need these when preparing fusible web for a project such as "Morning Light" on page 41. Designate a pair of scissors for paper cutting only. I like to use standard large-bladed scissors; however, some people prefer the smaller blades for detail cutting.

Marking pen or pencil. There are many on the market. For our purposes, we want something that will make marks that are visible on the gridded foundation. A regular pencil would be just fine. Don't use a ballpoint pen, however; the lines could bleed onto your project.

Iron. The iron is a big part of this process. I have two; the soleplate on my large iron measures $4\frac{3}{4}$" x $8\frac{3}{4}$", and my small travel iron measures $2\frac{7}{8}$" x $5\frac{1}{4}$". The small iron is handy for these projects, but either will work. Check the directions on your interfacing product for advice about temperature and the use of steam. Be careful not to touch the iron to the fusible glue on the gridded foundation. If that accidentally happens, there are products available to clean the iron. Or try one of the following methods that I use:

1. Put rubbing alcohol on a scrap of fabric or paper towel. Rub the hot iron plate on the fabric or paper towel in a circular motion to clean the surface.

2. Try a used fabric-softener dryer sheet. It looks a little like a piece of interfacing but is treated with fabric softener. Spray the sheet with a little water and run the hot iron plate over it until the surface of the iron is clean.

Appliqué or Teflon pressing sheet. This is a very slick sheet that will protect your iron from the fusible glue. I use it to cover the gridded fusible interfacing along the edge of the squares to prevent the iron from touching the fusible glue. Follow the manufacturer's instructions when using a pressing sheet.

Ironing board or ironing pad. You will need to fuse your fabrics in place frequently. It's best if you can work on an ironing board. (If you're fortunate, you'll have an oversized ironing board.) If you don't have an ironing board, you can use a portable ironing pad and slip it under your gridded foundation for the fusing process.

Fabric-basting glue. There are many glue sticks and fabric glues on the market. I usually use a basting glue that will wash out after the project is done. My favorite comes in a little plastic bottle and has a long, pointed nozzle.

Large sheets of white paper. These are very handy. Newspaper offices often sell the ends of newsprint rolls—nice large, clean, white paper on a roll for a reasonable price. You could also use plain butcher paper (without wax), or plain white wrapping paper. The paper has three purposes.

1. When placed underneath the gridded fusible foundation, it helps you see the lines.

2. It allows you to move your project without mishap; simply roll up the paper and quilt picture onto a wrapping-paper roll.

3. It protects your work surface during the fusing and gluing process.

Toothpicks. Plain wooden toothpicks are handy for nudging your little fabric pieces around and getting them aligned properly. The fibers on the wood grab the fabric fibers better than fingers do.

Basting spray. I use a basting spray to hold the backing, batting, and picture layers together so that they don't shift during the quilting process. If you choose to baste your quilt another way, you won't need this.

Pins—straight and basting. I use long, thin quilting pins to baste the tulle layer over the quilt picture. You can also use curved, rustproof safety pins.

Sewing machine. Your quilt picture will need to be machine quilted. You will also need a walking foot for straight-line quilting and a darning foot for free-motion quilting.

Threads. Pretty threads for quilting can add another design element to the quilt.

Tweezers. These are helpful for pulling loose threads through the tulle.

Fabric paints. I have tried several brands and they all worked well. You can even use regular acrylic paints if you mix them with a textile medium.

Beads. Beads are available in most craft stores, and the variety is inspiring. Use strong thread or a double thread to sew beads on by hand.

workplace choices

It is important to have a comfortable space in which to work. Everyone's home is different, and you will have to figure out what works best for you. Lighting is important in all stages of your project.

1. I work on a large ironing board surface. My husband made a large, removable plywood top for my regular ironing board, and I made a simple quilted cover for it. This large ironing surface is a very comfortable, useful place to work.

2. You may also use a regular ironing board. Although the area is smaller, it will still allow you to iron whenever you need to fuse the pieces.

3. You may work on a table and slide a portable ironing pad under your gridded fusible foundation for the fusing process. When doing so, just be careful that you don't dislodge any of the quilt pieces before they are fused.

prepare the gridded fusible foundation

It is very important that you prepare the gridded foundation properly. It's the foundation for your picture, and following the grid will enable you to get a good likeness. Several manufacturers make a fusible interfacing product with a printed grid. The product is available in various grid sizes. I use a 1" grid for my projects. Find a grid that has lines you can see well. Place the grid so that the fusible (bumpy) side is facing up. You'll be marking a bolder line at zero and every fifth line of the grid. You can mark a slightly bolder line or use a different color to mark the line. However, don't make the line so bold that it will show through your fabrics in the finished quilt picture. The lines on the marked foundation will match the lines on the photomap or the gridded transparency that you place over your own photo, as explained in "Prepare the Gridded Transparency" on page 16. The bolder lines allow you to easily keep or find your place.

The piece of gridded fusible foundation needs to be at least 1" larger than your project on all sides. Before you start, once again make sure that the bumpy or fusible side of the foundation is facing *up*. Run your fingernail over it and you will feel the bumps. You need to have the fusible side facing up for the fabric squares to adhere to the foundation.

To mark your gridded fusible foundation, follow these steps:

1. Place a sheet of white paper, slightly larger than the foundation, under the grid and pin along the sides in a few places to keep it from shifting.

2. Skip the square at the bottom left corner, and place a dot at the intersection of the bottom row and left column. Mark this dot number zero. This will leave an unused margin along the bottom and left side.

3. Using a pencil or marking pen, begin at the dot marked zero and mark every fifth vertical line so that you place marks at the 5", 10", 15", 20", and 25" lines (or more, depending on the diagram you're using).

4. Mark all the horizontal lines, beginning at zero and then at 5", 10", 15", and 20" or more. When you are finished, the layout of your gridded fusible foundation should be identical to the photomap or gridded transparency, except that the squares on the foundation will be larger.

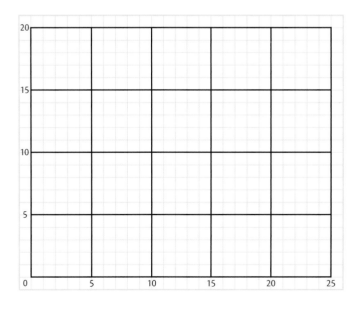

alternate gridded fusible interfacings

I have had difficulty finding the kind of gridded fusible interfacing I like, and you may also. Here are some suggestions for using what you find. Whichever product you choose, take the time to mark the foundation properly before you begin building the picture.

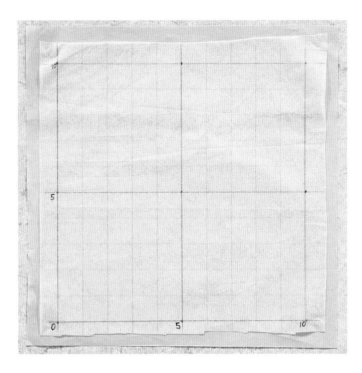
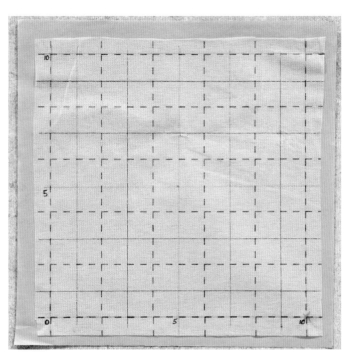

- **Fusible interfacing with preprinted 1" grid.** There are lots of 1" gridded fusible interfacings available, but the lines are hard to see. You can use these products if you put white paper underneath and have good lighting. Once you have marked the grid with a bold line every 5", it becomes easier to use. The example shown above has bold lines drawn with a regular graphite pencil.

- **Fusible interfacing with preprinted 2" grid.** There are also gridded fusible interfacings that have 2" grid lines instead of 1". Some of these products have highly visible lines. You could adapt these by drawing lines horizontally and vertically between the 2" grid lines to make 1" grid lines. Each 2" square will contain four 1" squares. This is very workable if you don't mind the extra marking. Sometimes just a dot in the middle of the 2" squares (to show where the 1"-square lines would intersect) is enough to keep you on track. The example shown above has 1" grid lines marked with a graphite pencil and 5" grid lines marked with bolder blue pencil.

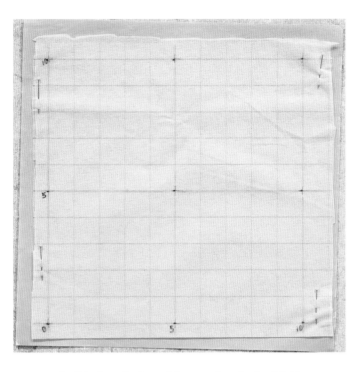

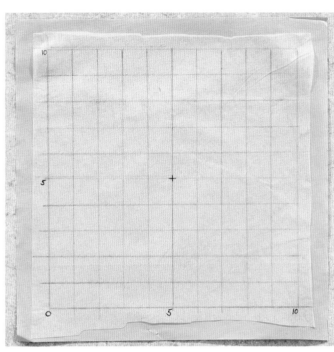

- **Nonfusible interfacing with preprinted 1" grid.** There is another interfacing product available that has bold lines and is a 1" grid. However, it's not fusible, and for this method we need a grid that is fusible. To make this product work, I purchased enough for my project and marked the bold lines every 5". Then I purchased enough plain, lightweight fusible interfacing to cover the entire grid. I placed the fusible interfacing on top of the gridded nonfusible interfacing and pinned along the edges so it wouldn't shift. I could see the grid lines through the fusible interfacing, so this actually worked pretty well. The gridded nonfusible interfacing does not get fused or glued to the picture and can be reused for your next project.

I recommend making a few registration marks on the fusible interfacing so that you can keep it aligned with the grid underneath. In the example above, the bottom grid layer is marked with blue lines every 5" and with small red crosses at the intersections. The top fusible interfacing layer has blue dots at every 5" intersection.

Note: Plain fusible interfacing is 22" wide. This means you will need twice as much yardage for projects wider than 20".

- **Fusible interfacing with hand-drawn grid.** The last option, which isn't really desirable, is to draw your own 1" grid on plain lightweight fusible interfacing. If you decide to do this, be sure to make all your lines consistent, and make a bolder line, or a line with a different color, every fifth square. In the example above, the 1" grid is drawn with a graphite pencil, and the 5" lines are drawn with a blue pencil.

The inspiration photo is underneath a gridded transparency overlay.

prepare the gridded transparency

Photomaps are provided for the projects in this book. However, if you are using your own photos, follow these steps to make a gridded transparency.

1. Select the correct transparency form on pages 61–63 for the size of your project. The number of squares on the form will determine the size of your quilt. For instance, form A is 25 squares wide and 20 squares high, or 25" x 20", which is the size of "Deep Blue Sea" on page 23. Form B is 35 squares wide and 25 squares high, or 35" x 25", like "Coastal Garden" on page 31. Form C will make a project 40" wide and 30" high, like "Pacific Beach" on page 37.

2. Take this book to a local copy shop and have the selected form photocopied onto acetate to make a transparency. At the same time, you may want to make a color copy of the inspiration photo for your project.

    Note: Be sure to enlarge your photo to exactly the same size as the form so that they will fit together as shown above.

3. Place the transparency over the photo so that the numbers are readable and aligned with the left and bottom edges of the photo. If you are using a photo with an obvious horizon line, such as "Pacific Beach," align the horizon with one of the lines on the gridded transparency. You may need to rotate the transparency slightly so that the horizon lines up with a grid line.

4. Use small pieces of removable tape on each side to secure the transparency over the photo so that it will not move.

5. This is your photo/transparency map. You will use the map as your guide to duplicate each square by placing fabric on the gridded foundation. The closer you match the colors and values shown on your map, the better your finished quilt picture will be.

choosing picture-quilt fabrics

Fabrics for picture quilts are chosen for the following characteristics:

- Color
- Value
- Visual texture (the pattern printed on the fabric)

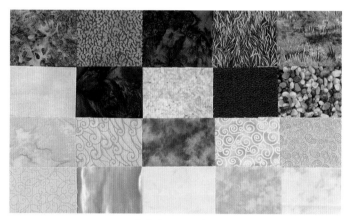

Fabric samples

When I select fabrics for a picture, I take the photo first to my stash and then to my local quilt shop. I try to find fabrics that have the same colors and values that I see in my photo. If I find the perfect fabric for the light part of the sky, I look for one or two additional fabrics that are very similar but with a little different print or swirl of color. I'm looking for variety, and I want them to blend. I want to be able to move from light to dark without abrupt changes. Do this with each section of your picture. Find fabrics for sky, water, land, trees, and whatever else you have in your photo.

When cut, some fabrics will show a white edge because the dye doesn't go all the way through the fibers. These fabrics are less desirable for your project, because the raw edges are more visible (especially on dark fabrics).

Sometimes you can use both sides of a print for different values. It might be dark gray on the right side and a lighter tone on the wrong side. Batiks are good if you can find the right shades and values. I use all kinds of fabrics: prints, batiks, hand-dyed solids, and tone-on-tones.

The variety adds to the interest of the finished picture. If you look closely at the photo of "Morning Light" on page 40, you will see music symbols below the cross. They represent me playing the piano! I often include music symbols in my quilts, because I love music. Can you see them in any of the other quilts? You might have some favorite things that you can include in subtle ways as small prints if they are the right color and value.

If you're purchasing fabrics, you need only small amounts of each. I usually buy ⅛ yard unless I have another use for a particular fabric; then I buy more. When I buy small amounts, I can purchase a greater variety. You might also have a good friend that will share some scraps with you.

There are many fabrics available that have actual rocks, leaves, grass, or other designs printed on them. When using these, remember that distant areas of the landscape should not show much detail. Fabrics with detail are best suited to the foreground of the quilt picture.

prewashing—should I or shouldn't I?

I *usually* prewash, for several reasons:

- It helps avoid bleeding. Any fabric that has dark, concentrated color, especially red or blue, may seep dye when it becomes wet. If it seeps onto another color, that can be very disappointing.

- It eliminates sizing in fabrics, which sometimes makes me sneeze.

- It ensures that I won't have surprises later on, when the quilt is laundered.

Press your fabric before cutting. A little spray starch is also a good idea, because it will firm up your fabric and make it easier to cut.

cutting picture-quilt fabrics

I've included a ¼" overlap on the squares—there is no seam allowance and no sewing. The fabrics are cut into 1¼" squares so that the gridded foundation will be completely covered and there won't be gaps between the squares.

1. Start in the lower-left corner of your photo, and select a group of assorted fabrics or scraps in the correct color family to match the photo.

2. Cut 1¼"-wide strips from the assorted fabrics.

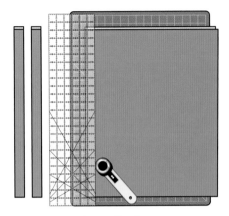

Cut 1¼" strips.

3. Lay several strips on your cutting mat, aligning the long sides as shown. (The strips don't need to be from the same fabric.) Crosscut the strips into 1¼" squares.

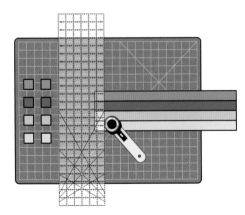

Cut 1¼" squares.

4. As you cut your fabrics, stack them in little piles on a tray or box lid.

Keep your fabric piles organized in color groups so that you can easily find the pieces you need. I often need more than one tray for all the fabrics. When I'm working on a fairly large project, I sometimes have three trays of fabric squares of different color groups.

You may try to cut all the fabrics for the whole picture at once, but I find that I have a better grasp of what I need if I cut as I work along the picture. I tend to cut groups of fabrics as I go; then I cut more if and when I need them.

placement of fabric squares

Although the gridded foundation has 1" squares, your fabric squares are cut oversized so that there won't be gaps between the squares. Position all the squares in the following manner:

1. Select a fabric square in the correct color and place it in the lower-left corner. Position it so that the top right corner of the fabric square aligns with the top right corner of the square on the gridded foundation as shown. The fabric square will overlap the line at the bottom of the first square by ¼" and the line at the left by ¼".

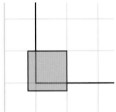

Align top right corners.

2. Place the second fabric square in the same manner, aligning the top right corners. The second square will overlap the first square by ¼". If you place all the fabric squares in this manner, all the overlaps will go in the same direction, and together the fabrics will look like little tiles on a roof. You may either move across your picture toward the right or move up toward the top. This will keep all the overlaps going in the same direction. If you were to move in other directions, your overlaps would start going in different directions and chaos would reign.

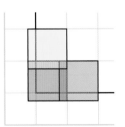

Overlap squares.

3. Continue adding squares. Check each square on your photomap and find a fabric that is as similar as possible to the color in your photo. Place the fabric on the corresponding square of the gridded foundation.

fusing as you go

When you have enough fabric squares in position for the base of your iron to fit over them, you'll want to fuse them in place. Always follow the manufacturer's instructions for the product you are using—each product is a little different, and the fusing time varies. Remember not to touch the fusible foundation (around the edges of the squares) with the iron, or you will get sticky residue on your iron. You can keep from ironing your fusible foundation by mistake if you use an appliqué or Teflon pressing sheet to cover the edges around the squares.

Working across the grid, press each section as you complete it to fuse the squares. I find that it's easiest if I move in sections across the picture all the way to the right-hand side. I usually work up and to the right, randomly adding squares but limiting myself to 10 squares vertically. I do not go farther up until I have completed the whole length of those 10 rows, all the way to the right-hand side. After they are cool, check that all the squares in those 10 rows are fused securely; if some are loose, iron over them again or use a little fabric glue.

As the picture gets larger, you will find it uncomfortable to reach up higher on the picture as you progress. You may want to drape the edge of the project over the side of the work surface. I do this by pulling the foundation, and the white paper that is under it, toward me so that about 8 completed rows are hanging off the edge of the table or board. I can then easily reach and continue on with the next 5 to 10 rows of the picture. When those rows are complete, I reposition the foundation and paper to reach the next section.

If you need to replace a square, carefully remove it, trying not to tear the interfacing. Replace the square, using a little fabric glue and tucking the new square under the edges of the adjoining squares. Any squares that do not adhere properly can be tacked down with a little fabric glue.

special-cut two-color squares

When you reach a place in the picture where a square has two colors, for instance, gray and brown, you will need to cut and glue. This happens where ocean meets rocks, trees meet sky, and so forth. In "Deep Blue Sea" on page 23, the special-cut two-color squares happen right at the beginning of the work, in the lower-left corner, between the sea and the grass. I find it helpful to draw the main lines on the gridded foundation with a marker so that I see the change coming ahead of time. The following steps will help you do this.

1. On a cutting mat, lay a whole fabric square of the underneath color (such as sea).

2. Select a square of the overlapping color (such as grass), and roughly cut away part of it to create the appropriate shape. Align the straight edges of the overlapping cut square with the edges of the whole underneath square.

3. Use a little fabric glue to adhere the cut square to the whole square to make a completed special-cut two-color square.

4. Position the new special-cut square in its correct place on the gridded foundation. It will later be fused to the foundation along with the other squares in the section.

5. Special cut the next two-color square so that it will fit together with the previous one. Remember that there is an extra ¼" on each fabric square that is hidden from view. It can be a little confusing when you first start cutting and fitting the two-color fabric squares together. Once you've done three or four squares, you'll see how they fit together and it'll become easier. Cut the overlapping square, lay it on the whole square, see if they fit correctly, trim if needed, and then glue.

Continue working up and across the picture, from the left to the right, varying the fabrics as you go to make your quilt look as much like the inspiration photo as possible.

sky treatments

The process for making the sky is the same. As you look at the "Pacific Beach" inspiration photo on page 37, you will notice that the sky moves from lighter at the bottom to darker at the top. I tried to gently move from lights to mediums as I moved up. There is also a white cloud to work in.

As you move from color to color in whole squares, add special-cut two-color squares to soften the cloud shapes. You can also soften the edges of clouds after completing the quilt picture, if you wish, by going back and adding some paint to the edges of the clouds, overlaying long shapes of fabric cut freehand and glued, or overlaying scraps of polyester stuffing over the cloud area before adding the tulle layer.

completing the picture quilt

When your picture is completely done and all the squares are fused down, stand back and look at it from a distance. You can also look through a reducing glass, reverse magnifier, or peephole device made for a door—all of which make objects that are close appear as though they're far away. Note the areas where you want to add or change something that doesn't please your eye. Then decide how to accomplish what you want. Dabs of paint might enhance something that you want to change slightly. You can also cut some fabrics freehand and glue them over an area of the quilt picture. In "Morning Light" on page 41, I added some thin lines of clouds by cutting and laying fabrics over the other sky fabrics. In "Pacific Beach," I special cut some splashes, and then added a little white fabric paint. I suggest that you use paint sparingly, because you don't want to distract from the patchwork feel of your work.

tulle overlay

Another unusual thing about this picture-quilt technique is the tulle overlay. Before you add the tulle layer, you can adorn the top of the fabric picture with additional embellishments, such as little rocks, tiny sticks, and dried flowers, which you quilt around. After deciding where I want a rock, I place it between the fabric picture layer and the tulle overlay and then surround it with pins to hold it in place. Then I quilt a line around the rock, as close to it as I can, to secure it. The tulle holds the rock in place. After the quilting is complete, you can add more embellishments, such as beads or dimensional flowers, on top of the tulle. Sew beads on by hand with a strong thread.

tulle—what is it?

Tulle is very fine netting that is often used for bridal veils and formal wear. I use it because I'm building a picture with many little pieces of fabric that have raw edges. When I cover the picture with tulle, it holds down all those little raw edges. The tulle over the picture also blends the colors.

I purchase tulle in 45" or 72" widths, and I have found it in many different colors. I use black tulle on most of my pictures. I have tried some others colors as well: teal, blue, copper, and peach. Some tulle has a sparkle that adds a nice extra touch to the picture. I especially like the sparkle for pictures with water in them. For the most part, the tulle will simply not show. Most people are surprised when you mention that it's there; they just don't see the tulle until it's pointed out. I've found that the darker tulle colors usually work best. In the example below, you can see that the fabric colors show through but are altered slightly, depending on which color of tulle is over them.

White   Teal   Yellow   Black   Copper   Peach   Blue

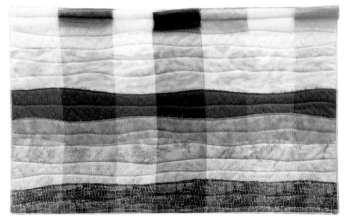

Strips of tulle in different colors have been laid over the landscape fabrics to show you the effect. Along the top are several thicknesses of each tulle to show its color.

using your own photos

Before using your own photos, I recommend that you do at least one project in this book to familiarize yourself with the techniques. There are several things you need to consider when using your own photos.

- Avoid copyright infringement. It is *very* important that you do not use photos out of magazines, books, or even from the Internet unless you contact the photographer and get permission to do so.

- I recommend using photos that either you have taken or a family member has taken. If you want to use someone else's photo, take the steps to contact them and get permission in writing before you start the project.

- It is best to use photos that have only a few, simple elements in them for this style of quilt. If there are flowers, houses, or details that are hard to duplicate in this manner, consider a fusible appliqué over the top of the patchwork background.

- Go through your photos and find a picture that you think is especially beautiful. I enjoy using photos of places that have special meaning in my life. It is much more fun to work on a project that you are going to love to display when it's complete. Your favorite places will remind you of warm fuzzy feelings.

- Remember to enlarge your photo to the size of the transparency forms.

- Decide how large you want the quilt to be and use the correct transparency form for that size.

- The yardages listed in each project are for quilts of that size and can be used as a guide for backing, binding, and batting. If you use your own photo to create a quilt of the same size, you will need to estimate yardage for the picture portion of your quilt.

"My View of College Cove" by Edith L. Harmer. Edith used an enlarged snapshot of one of her favorite beach scenes. I think it's lovely. This was her first attempt at this landscape method.

DEEP BLUE SEA

by Pat Durbin

*This coastal shot showcases the deep colors
of the ocean. When looking at this quilt,
I remember the peace of walking on the beach.*

Inspiration photo

FINISHED QUILT SIZE: 25" X 20"
TOTAL NUMBER OF PIECES: 500
SKILL LEVEL: BEGINNER

FABRIC SELECTION

Use the photo to select fabrics to match the
colors and values. Notice, for instance, that the
ocean color is blue, but there are various shades
and tones of blue and teal. The rocks and grass in
the foreground can show more detail. If you have
some grass print fabrics, this is a nice place to use
them. Variety in each color group will enrich the
patchwork and painted feel of your picture.

materials

All yardages are based on 42"-wide fabrics, unless otherwise noted.

⅓ yard *total* of assorted blue and teal scraps for ocean

¼ yard *total* of assorted light blue scraps for sky

¼ yard *total* of assorted bright green scraps for grass

¼ yard *total* of assorted white scraps for clouds

⅛ yard *total* of assorted dark green scraps for trees and shrubs

⅛ yard *total* of assorted tan and gray scraps for sand

⅛ yard *total* of assorted black and dark gray scraps for rocks

¼ yard of dark blue fabric for binding

1 yard of fabric for backing and hanging sleeve

29" x 24" piece of batting

¾ yard of gridded fusible interfacing

¾ yard of black or blue tulle

28" x 23" piece of plain white paper

Optional embellishments: white acrylic fabric paints, scraps of polyester fiberfill stuffing for clouds, clear or white beads (about ⅛")

cutting

For detailed instructions, refer to "Cutting Picture-Quilt Fabrics" on page 18.

Assorted Scraps	How Used	Number to Cut	Size to Cut
Blue and teal	Ocean	180	1¼" x 1¼"
Light blue	Sky	150	1¼" x 1¼"
Bright green	Grass	85	1¼" x 1¼"
White	Clouds	75	1¼" x 1¼"
Dark green	Trees/shrubs	50	1¼" x 1¼"
Tan and gray	Sand	35	1¼" x 1¼"
Black and dark gray	Rocks	30	1¼" x 1¼"
From the backing fabric, cut: 1 piece, 24" x 29"			
From the dark blue fabric, cut: 3 strips, 2¼" x 42"			

preparing the foundation

For detailed instructions, refer to "Prepare the Gridded Fusible Foundation" on page 13.

Cut a piece of gridded fusible interfacing at least 27" x 22". Use a pencil or marking pen to mark bold lines every five squares on the gridded foundation as shown below.

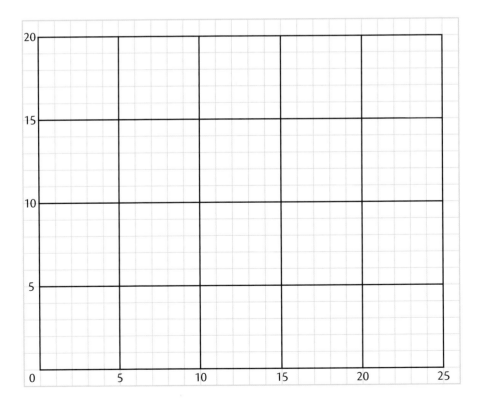

building the picture

For detailed instructions, refer to "Placement of Fabric Squares" on page 18 and "Special-Cut Two-Color Squares" on page 19.

1. Refer to the photomap on page 56 when selecting fabric squares for your grid. The better you can duplicate the colors and values of the photomap, the better your finished project will be. Start with the colors in the lower-left corner; in this case, that will be the rock colors and then the grassy greens. Working one 5" x 5" section of the grid at a time, build your picture by following the photomap, moving from left to right and from bottom to top. You'll need whole 1¼" squares as well as two-color squares for this first section. Shaping these two-color squares will give definition to the quilt picture, creating a sharper image.

2. As you encounter areas where there are darker or lighter colors, use the darker or lighter fabrics from the variety of cut squares.

3. Complete the first 5" x 5" section, and then move to the next 5" x 5" section to the right. Complete columns 6–10, columns 11–15, and so forth. Fuse the fabrics as you complete each section. Continue until you have completed a section five rows high all the way across to column 25. Be sure that all the sections are fused. Refer to "Fusing as You Go" on page 19 as needed.

4. Pull the picture toward you until the next five rows are easily reached. Place and fuse rows 6–10 in the same manner, all the way across to column 25. Be sure the fused squares are adhered. If not, press areas as needed or use a little fabric glue.

5. Repeat steps 1–4, working five rows at a time across the width of the picture and progressing toward the top until the quilt picture is complete.

embellishing

Look at your quilt picture from a distance and note any areas you would like to improve. You can embellish your quilt top as desired with paint, extra tulle, or stuffing.

1. Use a sponge to dab on some white fabric paint to soften the edges of the clouds. Use just a little; it's easy to add more if desired, but you can't remove it if you've used too much. You can also cut fabric shapes and use them to shape cloud edges.

2. White paint can be applied sparingly for the foam along the edges of the water. After the quilting is completed, clear or white beads can be stitched on the outside of the tulle to add sparkle.

3. If desired, you can do additional embellishing after you've layered the quilt picture with batting and backing. Then tear little pieces of polyester stuffing and lay them over the fabric clouds to add a little airiness to the clouds' appearance before adding the tulle layer.

finishing

For detailed instructions, refer to "Finishing Techniques" on page 45.

1. Layer the quilt picture with batting and backing; baste the layers together. Place the tulle on top and baste in place.

2. Machine quilt as desired. I quilted lines in an up-and-down design to enhance the close-up grass appearance. Then I quilted smooth curves over most of the sea area, with a few feathered shapes over the white foam, and quilted zigzag lines to give the impression of distant trees on the mountains.

3. Mark a cutting line around the outside edges to straighten the sides and square up the corners. To prevent the outside edges from stretching, attach the binding before you trim the excess fabric.

4. Use the 2¼"-wide dark blue strips to bind the edges.

5. Add a hanging sleeve using the same fabric as the backing.

6. Attach a signature label to your work of art.

A TIME TO SOW

by Pat Durbin

While traveling through the Midwest in the spring-time, my husband snapped many landscape shots for me. This simple scene shows the plowed fields ready for planting and the clear green of winter wheat in the distance. The bounty of the farmlands will come to full bloom later in the year.

Inspiration photo

FINISHED QUILT SIZE: 25" X 20"
TOTAL NUMBER OF PIECES: 500
SKILL LEVEL: BEGINNER

FABRIC SELECTION

When using the photo to select fabrics to match the colors and values, notice that there are various shades and tones of brown in the plowed ground. Variety in each color group will enrich the patchwork and painted feel of your picture.

materials

All yardages are based on 42"-wide fabrics, unless otherwise noted.

¼ yard *total* of assorted brown and tan scraps for ground

¼ yard *total* of assorted bright green scraps for grasses

¼ yard *total* of assorted blue scraps for sky

¼ yard *total* of assorted white scraps for clouds

⅛ yard *total* of assorted dark green scraps for trees

¼ yard of brown-and-green striped fabric for flange

¼ yard of brown fabric for binding

1 yard of fabric for backing and hanging sleeve

29" x 24" piece of batting

¾ yard of gridded fusible interfacing

¾ yard of black tulle

28" x 23" piece of plain white paper

Optional embellishments: white, light green, and yellow acrylic fabric paints; scraps of polyester fiberfill stuffing for clouds

cutting

For detailed instructions, refer to "Cutting Picture-Quilt Fabrics" on page 18.

Assorted Scraps	How Used	Number to Cut	Size to Cut
Brown and tan	Ground	150	1¼" x 1¼"
Bright green	Grasses	125	1¼" x 1¼"
Blue	Sky	125	1¼" x 1¼"
White	Clouds	125	1¼" x 1¼"
Dark green	Trees	50	1¼" x 1¼"
From the backing fabric, cut: 1 piece, 24" x 29"			
From the brown-and-green striped fabric, cut: 3 strips, 1¼" x 42"			
From the brown fabric, cut: 3 strips, 2¼" x 42"			

preparing the foundation

For detailed instructions, refer to "Prepare the Gridded Fusible Foundation" on page 13.

Cut a piece of gridded fusible interfacing at least 27" x 22". Use a pencil or marking pen to mark bold lines every five squares on the gridded foundation as shown below.

building the picture

For detailed instructions, refer to "Placement of Fabric Squares" on page 18 and "Special-Cut Two-Color Squares" on page 19.

1. Refer to the photomap on page 57 when selecting fabric squares for your grid. The better you can duplicate the colors and values of the photomap, the better your finished project will be. Start with the colors in the lower-left corner; in this case, that will be the grassy greens. Working one 5" x 5" section of the grid at a time, build your picture by following the photomap, moving from left to right and from bottom to top. You'll need whole 1¼" squares as well as two-color squares for this first section. After completing the transition from grass to plowed ground, you may cut some special spiked-grass sections and use fabric glue to adhere them over the line to soften the edges.

2. As you encounter areas where there are darker or lighter colors, use the darker or lighter fabrics from the variety of cut squares.

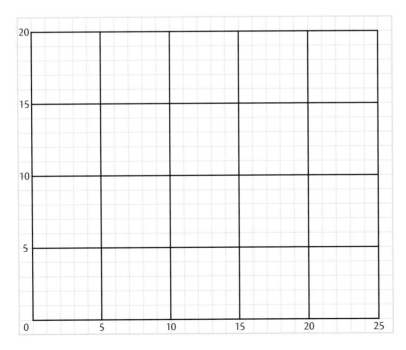

3. Complete the first 5" x 5" section, and then move to the next 5" x 5" section to the right. Complete columns 6–10, columns 11–15, and so forth. Fuse the fabrics as you complete each section. Continue until you have completed a section five rows high all the way across to column 25. Be sure that all the sections are fused. Refer to "Fusing as You Go" on page 19 as needed.

4. Pull the picture toward you until the next five rows are easily reached. Place and fuse rows 6–10 in the same manner, all the way across to column 25. Be sure the fused squares are adhered. If not, press areas as needed or use a little fabric glue.

5. Repeat steps 1–4, working five rows at a time across the width of the picture and progressing toward the top until the quilt picture is complete. Note that the tree near the center is added after the background is complete (see step 2 of "Embellishing," below).

embellishing

Look at your quilt picture from a distance and note any areas you would like to improve. You can embellish your quilt top as desired with paint, extra tulle, or stuffing.

1. Use a sponge to dab on some white fabric paint to soften the edges of the clouds. Use just a little; it's easy to add more if desired, but you can't remove it if you've used too much. You can also cut fabric shapes and attach them with fabric glue to shape cloud edges.

2. To make the tree near the center, use the picture as a guide to cut some trunk and limb shapes. Use fabric glue to adhere them over the background. Then use a brush or sponge to apply a little light green paint over the background. Leave some blank spots. I added a few spots of light yellow over the green for highlights.

3. If desired, you can do additional embellishing after you've layered the quilt picture with batting and backing. Then tear little pieces of polyester stuffing and lay them over the fabric clouds to add a little airiness to the clouds' appearance before adding the tulle layer.

finishing

For detailed instructions, refer to "Finishing Techniques" on page 45.

1. Layer the quilt picture with batting and backing; baste the layers together. Place the tulle on top and baste in place.

2. Machine quilt as desired. I quilted zigzag lines to enhance the center grass line and the special green tree.

3. Mark a cutting line around the outside edges to straighten the sides and square up the corners. To prevent the outside edges from stretching, attach the binding before you trim the excess fabric.

4. To add a flange or flat piping border, refer to "Optional Flange," below.

5. Use the 2¼" brown strips to bind the edges.

6. Add a hanging sleeve using the same fabric as the backing.

7. Attach a signature label to your work of art.

OPTIONAL FLANGE

The flange or flat piping is an optional strip that adds another color opportunity or design touch. Cut enough 1¼" x 42" strips to go around the perimeter of your quilt (for this project, you'll need three or four strips). They may be pieced if necessary. Fold the strips in half lengthwise, wrong sides together, and press. Measure the quilt picture through the center from top to bottom and cut two strips to fit that measurement. Align the long raw edges of the cut strips with the marked line and baste the strips to the side edges using a scant ¼"-wide seam allowance.

Measure the quilt picture through the center from side to side and cut two strips to fit that measurement. Align the long raw edges of the cut strips with the marked line and baste the strips to the top and bottom edges.

COASTAL GARDEN

by Pat Durbin

*We discovered a beautiful sanctuary overlooking
the ocean, just a step up from the beach.
Here is God's hand at work again—wonderful!
My husband, Gary, took this photo.*

Inspiration photo

FINISHED QUILT SIZE: 35" X 25"
TOTAL NUMBER OF PIECES: 875
SKILL LEVEL: INTERMEDIATE
SPECIAL FEATURES: FUSIBLE GRASS APPLIQUÉS
AND DIMENSIONAL FLOWERS

FABRIC SELECTION

As you select fabrics to match the colors and values you see in the photo, notice the various shades and tones of blue and white in the sky. The greens vary from bright to dark. Variety in each color group will enrich the patchwork and painted feel of your picture.

The bush in the picture is an azalea. I couldn't find a fabric with this flower, so I substituted one that I thought was pretty. Choose one or two fabrics that are completely covered with flowers and leaves; you don't want any background showing around the flowers. The fabric needs to look like a real part of a bush. I also used a fabric with rosebuds on it for the small flowers in the foreground, just to the left of the center. I fussy cut around the buds and leaves and glued them over the grassy greens.

materials

All yardages are based on 42"-wide fabrics, unless otherwise noted.

½ yard *total* of assorted blue, light blue, and white scraps for sky

³/₈ yard *total* of assorted florals for flower bush

¼ yard *total* of assorted medium to dark blue scraps for ocean

¼ yard *total* of assorted green scraps for shrubs

¼ yard *total* of assorted bright green scraps for grasses

⅛ yard of rosebud print for flower appliqués

⅓ yard of dark blue fabric for binding

1¼ yards of fabric for backing and hanging sleeve

39" x 29" piece of batting

⅞ yard of gridded fusible interfacing

⅞ yard of black or dark blue tulle

38" x 28" piece of plain white paper

15" x 8" piece of paper-backed fusible web for grass appliqués

Optional embellishments: light and medium pink acrylic fabric paints, beads (about ⅛"), scraps of white organza for clouds

cutting

For detailed instructions, refer to "Cutting Picture-Quilt Fabrics" on page 18.

Assorted Scraps	How Used	Number to Cut	Size to Cut
Blue, light blue, and white	Sky	350	1¼" x 1¼"
Florals	Flower bush	235	1¼" x 1¼"
Medium to dark blue	Ocean	135	1¼" x 1¼"
Green	Shrubs	125	1¼" x 1¼"
Bright greens	Grasses	100	1¼" x 1¼"
From the backing fabric, cut: 1 piece, 39" x 29"			
From the dark blue fabric, cut: 4 strips, 2¼" x 42"			

preparing the foundation

For detailed instructions, refer to "Prepare the Gridded Fusible Foundation" on page 13.

Cut a piece of gridded fusible interfacing at least 37" x 27". Use a pencil or marking pen to mark bold lines every five squares on the gridded foundation as shown below.

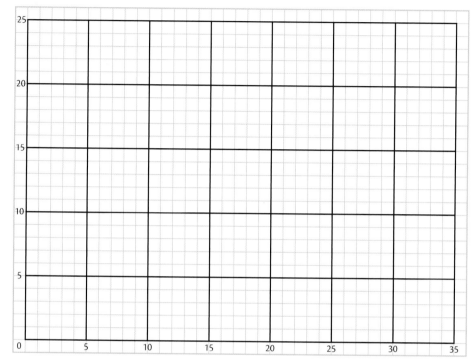

building the picture

For detailed instructions, refer to "Placement of Fabric Squares" on page 18 and "Special-Cut Two-Color Squares" on page 19.

1. Refer to the photomap on page 58 when selecting fabric squares for your grid. The better you can duplicate the colors and values of the photomap, the better your finished project will be. Start with the colors in the lower-left corner; in this case, that will be the grassy greens. Notice that the grasses have lighter and darker tones. The flowery bush is created from squares; later you'll add fussy-cut shapes along the edges where the bush meets the grass, ocean, and sky. Working one 5" x 5" section of the grid at a time, build your picture by following the photomap, moving from left to right and from bottom to top. You'll need whole 1¼" squares as well as two-color squares for this first section. Most of the two-color squares go where the shrubs overlap the ocean and sky. Shaping these two-color squares will give definition to the quilt picture, creating a sharper image.

2. As you encounter areas where there are darker or lighter colors, use the darker or lighter fabrics from the variety of cut squares.

3. Complete the first 5" x 5" section, and then move to the next 5" x 5" section to the right. Complete columns 6–10, columns 11–15, and so forth. Fuse the fabrics as you complete each section. Continue until you have completed a section five rows high all the way across to column 35. Be sure that all the sections are fused. Refer to "Fusing as You Go" on page 19 as needed.

4. Pull the picture toward you until the next five rows are easily reached. Place and fuse rows 6 to 10 in the same manner, all the way across to column 35. Be sure the fused squares are adhered. If not, press areas as needed or use a little fabric glue.

5. Repeat steps 1–4, working five rows at a time across the width of the picture and progressing toward the top until the quilt picture is complete.

embellishing

Look at your quilt picture from a distance and note any areas you would like to improve. You can embellish your quilt top as desired with paint, extra tulle, or stuffing.

1. For the distant flower bushes near the center, use paint and the tip of a brush to make light and medium pink dots.

2. From the white organza, cut a few cloud shapes and use a little fabric glue to adhere the shapes over the sky to enhance the appearance of the clouds.

3. To make the long grasses in the foreground, do the following:

   - From the paper-backed fusible web, cut three to four pieces, about 4" x 8".

   - On the *wrong* side of a grassy green scrap, place a piece of fusible web on the bias (diagonally, not on the straight grain or edge), and fuse in place.

   - Varying the length and width of each wedge, cut out several long wedges of grass about 3/16" at the widest end and tapering to a point. Remove the paper backing.

   - Place the web side down and position a grass wedge on your quilt picture, referring to the photo on page 30 as needed. Place the tip of the iron on the base of the wedge. Move the grass to the right or left as you slowly iron up the length of it. You'll be able to manipulate the grass because it has been cut on the bias. You can curve and tip the grasses as desired.

4. To make the small flower bush in the foreground (just left of the center), fussy cut 9 to 10 flowers and leaves from the rosebud print. (The exact number you'll need will depend on your fabric

and how many flowers you want on the bush.) Use fabric glue to adhere the pieces to the quilt picture, referring to the photo as needed.

finishing

For detailed instructions, refer to "Finishing Techniques" on page 45.

1. Layer the quilt picture with batting and backing; baste the layers together. Place the tulle on top and baste in place.

2. Machine quilt as desired. I quilted some leaf shapes in the bushes and additional grass shapes along the bottom.

3. Mark a cutting line around the outside edges to straighten the sides and square up the corners. To prevent the outside edges from stretching, attach the binding before you trim the excess fabric.

4. Use the 2¼"-wide dark blue strips to bind the edges.

5. After the quilting is completed, you may want to add more embellishments. Beads can be stitched on the outside of the tulle to add sparkle. You can also add a few beads for flower centers. Refer to "Adding Dimensional Flowers" above right to create a few flowers and leaves.

6. Add a hanging sleeve using the same fabric as the backing.

7. Attach a signature label to your work of art.

ADDING DIMENSIONAL FLOWERS

1. Iron paper-backed fusible web to the wrong side of a small floral scrap.

2. Remove the paper backing and fuse the piece to the wrong side of another floral scrap. Now the fusible web is sandwiched between two pieces of fabric.

3. Use the fused two-sided floral fabric to fussy cut several individual flower shapes or leaves. (The exact number will depend on your fabric and how many flowers you want to add to the bush.)

4. Use an iron to apply heat to the flower or leaf shape. While it's hot, bend the flower or leaf to make a dimensional shape; hold until it's cool. The flower or leaf will hold its new shape.

5. Make a few stitches by hand or machine in the center of the flower or leaf shape to attach it to the quilt picture.

PACIFIC BEACH

by Pat Durbin

One of our favorite places to visit is Dry Lagoon
State Park, north of Trinidad, California. We
walk there and hunt for agates. Wonderful
memories are stitched into this quilt. This is
another photo taken my husband, Gary.

Inspiration photo

FINISHED QUILT SIZE: 40" X 30"
TOTAL NUMBER OF PIECES: 1200
SKILL LEVEL: INTERMEDIATE
SPECIAL FEATURES: TINY ROCKS ON
BEACH AREA UNDER TULLE

FABRIC SELECTION

When using the photo to select fabrics to match
the colors and values, notice that there are
various shades and tones of blue and teal in
the ocean. The sand colors range from light to
medium. Variety in each color group will enrich
the patchwork and painted feel of your picture.
More is better.

materials

All yardages are based on 42"-wide fabrics, unless otherwise noted.

$^2/_3$ yard *total* of assorted light blue scraps for sky

$^1/_2$ yard *total* of assorted black and dark gray scraps for rocks

$^1/_2$ yard *total* of assorted blue and teal scraps for ocean

$^1/_3$ yard *total* of assorted white scraps for sea foam

$^1/_3$ yard *total* of assorted tan and gray scraps for sand

$^1/_3$ yard of dark blue fabric for binding

$1^5/_8$ yards of fabric for backing and hanging sleeve

44" x 34" piece of batting

$1^1/_3$ yards of gridded fusible interfacing

$1^1/_4$ yards of black or dark blue tulle

43" x 33" piece of plain white paper

Optional embellishments: white acrylic fabric paint, clear or white beads (about $^1/_8$"), tiny rocks, small pieces of driftwood

cutting

For detailed instructions, refer to "Cutting Picture-Quilt Fabrics" on page 18.

Assorted Scraps	How Used	Number to Cut	Size to Cut
Light blue	Sky	500	1¼" x 1¼"
Black and dark gray	Rocks	300	1¼" x 1¼"
Blue and teal	Ocean	350	1¼" x 1¼"
White	Sea foam	175	1¼" x 1¼"
Tan and gray	Sand	210	1¼" x 1¼"
From the backing fabric, cut: 1 piece, 44" x 34"			
From the dark blue fabric, cut: 4 strips, 2¼" x 42"			

preparing the foundation

For detailed instructions, refer to "Prepare the Gridded Fusible Foundation" on page 13.

Cut a piece of gridded fusible interfacing at least 42" x 32". Use a pencil or marking pen to mark bold lines every five squares on the gridded foundation as shown below.

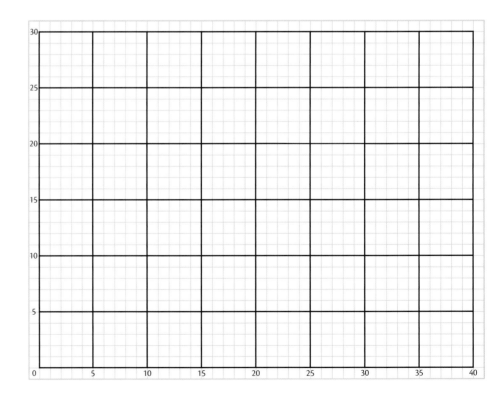

building the picture

For detailed instructions, refer to "Placement of Fabric Squares" on page 18 and "Special-Cut Two-Color Squares" on page 19.

1. Refer to the photomap on page 59 when selecting fabric squares for your grid. Start with the colors in the lower-left corner; in this case, that will be the sand and then rock colors. Notice that the sand colors change from lighter to darker tones. The rocks will need a variety of dark gray to blacks as well. Working one 5" x 5" section of the grid at a time, build your picture by following the photomap, moving from left to right and from bottom to top. You'll need whole 1¼" squares as well as two-color squares for this first section. Shaping these two-color squares will give definition to the quilt picture, creating a sharper image.

2. As you encounter areas where there are darker or lighter colors, use the darker or lighter fabrics from the variety of cut squares.

3. Complete the first 5" x 5" section, and then move to the next 5" x 5" section to the right. Complete columns 6–10, columns 11–15, and so forth. Fuse the fabrics as you complete each section. Continue until you have completed a section five rows high all the way across to column 40. Be sure that all the sections are fused. Refer to "Fusing as You Go" on page 19 as needed.

4. Pull the picture toward you until the next five rows are easily reached. Place and fuse rows 6–10 in the same manner, all the way across to column 40. Be sure the fused squares are adhered. If not, press areas as needed or use a little fabric glue.

5. Repeat steps 1–4, working five rows at a time across the width of the picture and progressing toward the top until the quilt picture is complete.

embellishing

Look at your quilt picture from a distance and note any areas you would like to improve. You can embellish your quilt top as desired with paint, extra tulle, or stuffing.

1. Use a sponge to dab on some white fabric paint to add some shape to the foam and a light splash where appropriate. Use just a light hand; it's easy to add more if desired, but you can't remove it if you've used too much. You can also cut fabric shapes and use them to create water splashes.

2. Tiny rocks and driftwood can be added under the tulle on the sand area and stitched around during the quilting process. Stitch a line of quilting and then place a rock near it. For the next stitching, get as close as you can without hitting the rock.

3. After the quilting is completed, clear or white beads can be stitched on the outside of the tulle to add sparkle.

finishing

For detailed instructions, refer to "Finishing Techniques" on page 45.

1. Layer the quilt picture with batting and backing; baste the layers together. Place the tulle on top and baste in place.

2. Machine quilt as desired. I quilted wavy shapes in the water to enhance the appearance of movement.

3. Mark a cutting line around the outside edges to straighten the sides and square up the corners. To prevent the outside edges from stretching, attach the binding before you trim the excess fabric.

4. Use the 2¼"-wide dark blue strips to bind the edges.

5. Add a hanging sleeve using the same fabric as the backing.

6. Attach a signature label to your work of art.

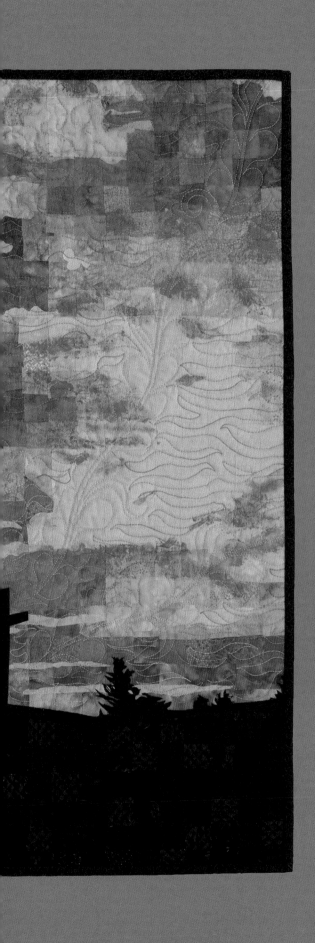

MORNING LIGHT

by Pat Durbin

This is the view from my dining room window on a particularly beautiful dawn. It's so lovely to enjoy God's handiwork early in the morning. This photo was taken by my husband, Gary.

Inspiration photo

FINISHED QUILT SIZE: 40" X 30"
TOTAL NUMBER OF PIECES: 1200
SKILL LEVEL: INTERMEDIATE
SPECIAL FEATURES: FUSIBLE APPLIQUÉD TREES,
CHURCH ROOF, AND CROSS

FABRIC SELECTION

The sky has a section of bright orange and yellow and then a section where the shades are much softer. Variety in each color group will enrich the painted feel of your picture. The section below the tree line features many black squares. I used one single black fabric for the appliquéd trees, church roof, and cross. (Notice the black with music symbols near the center—that represents me playing the piano. Can you hear the music?)

materials

All yardages are based on 42"-wide fabrics, unless otherwise noted.

²⁄₃ yard *total* of assorted orange and yellow scraps for clouds

²⁄₃ yard *total* of assorted light blue scraps for sky

½ yard *total* of assorted purple and gray scraps for clouds

⅓ yard *total* of assorted black scraps for foreground

½ yard of black fabric for trees, church roof, and cross

1⅓ yards of fusible web for trees, church roof, and cross

1⅝ yards of fabric for backing and hanging sleeve

⅓ yard of black fabric for binding

44" x 34" piece of batting

1⅓ yards of gridded fusible inter-facing

1¼ yards of black tulle

43" x 33" piece of plain white paper

Tracing paper

Optional embellishments: blue-gray acrylic fabric paints, yellow tulle

cutting

For detailed instructions, refer to "Cutting Picture-Quilt Fabrics" on page 18.

Assorted Scraps	How Used	Number to Cut	Size to Cut
Orange and yellow	Clouds	500	1¼" x 1¼"
Light blue	Sky	500	1¼" x 1¼"
Purple and gray	Clouds	300	1¼" x 1¼"
Black	Foreground	200	1¼" x 1¼"
From the backing fabric, cut: 1 piece, 44" x 34"			
From the black fabric for binding, cut: 4 strips, 2¼" x 42"			

preparing the foundation

For detailed instructions, refer to "Prepare the Gridded Fusible Foundation" on page 13.

Cut a piece of gridded fusible interfacing at least 42" x 32". Use a pencil or marking pen to mark bold lines every five squares on the gridded foundation as shown below.

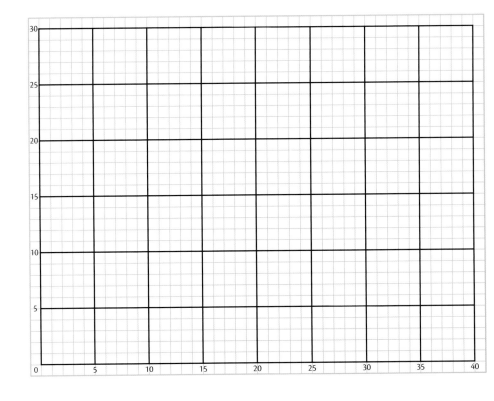

building the picture

For detailed instructions, refer to "Placement of Fabric Squares" on page 18 and "Special-Cut Two-Color Squares" on page 19.

1. Refer to the photomap on page 60 when selecting fabric squares for your grid. The better you can duplicate the colors and values of the photomap, the better your finished project will be. Start with the colors in the lower-left corner; in this case, that will be the black and then bright yellow and orange. Working one 5" x 5" section of the grid at a time, build your picture by following the photomap, moving from left to right and from bottom to top. You'll need mostly whole 1¼" squares for this first section.

   Complete the section of black up to where the tree shapes begin. Then switch to the sky colors. The fusible trees, church roof, and cross will be appliquéd over the top of the bright sky so that the sky can show through (see step 8 on page 44). For the sky area, you'll need whole 1¼" squares and special-cut two-color squares to shape clouds.

2. As you encounter areas where there are darker or lighter colors, use the darker or lighter fabrics from the variety of cut squares.

3. Complete the first 5" x 5" section, and then move to the next 5" x 5" section to the right. Complete columns 6–10, columns 11–15, and so forth. Fuse the fabrics as you complete each section. Continue until you have completed a section five rows high all the way across to column 40. Be sure that all the sections are fused. Refer to "Fusing as You Go" on page 19 as needed.

4. Pull the picture toward you until the next five rows are easily reached. Place and fuse rows 6–10 in the same manner, all the way across to column 40. Be sure the fused squares are adhered. If not, press areas as needed or use a little fabric glue.

5. Repeat steps 1–4, working five rows at a time across the width of the picture and progressing toward the top until the quilt picture is complete.

adding the trees, church roof, and cross

1. Place tracing paper over the photomap; use tape to secure the tracing paper in place. On the paper, make a mark to indicate the bottom corners of the photo and write "right side." Draw a line about ½" below where you ended the black squares in step 1 of "Building the Picture." This will be the starting point for your appliqué overlay. Trace the edge of the tree line with a pencil, making the lines dark enough to be easily seen. (Don't try to trace every little tree detail—an impression of the shape is what you need.) Then, draw a few holes in the trees where the light shows through. As you continue over to the cross and roof line, use a ruler to make your lines straight. Then trace the grid lines covering the trees, church roof, and cross.

   Note: The vertical section of the cross is parallel to the edge of the quilt, but the crossbar is not parallel to the bottom edge. This is because of the angle of the shot. You need to maintain that angle to get a good perspective in your piece.

2. To make a reverse image for the paper-backed fusible web, turn the tracing over. If the pencil line isn't dark enough to see the image clearly from this side, use a window or light box to trace the line to darken it. This will be the "wrong side" of the paper.

3. Draw enough grid lines on the wrong side of the paper to cover the traced lines of the trees, church roof, and cross.

4. Cut a piece of paper-backed fusible web about 41" long. Draw a 1" grid on the paper side of the fusible web. You'll only need to draw enough of the grid to cover the area represented by the trees and roof outline. Refer to the pencil-tracing map from step 3 as needed.

5. Use the pencil-tracing map as a guide to sketch the cutting line onto the paper side of the fusible web. Look at each little square and enlarge that portion of the tree outline to fit in the square on the fusible web. Take your time, and remember it doesn't have to be exact.

6. When you have drawn the entire silhouette, cut out the shape, leaving a margin that is approximately ½" wide outside the drawn line.

   Note: Remember that the image is reversed, so the building is on the left.

7. Following the manufacturer's instructions for the fusible web, fuse the tree-outline shape to the wrong side of the black fabric. Carefully cut out the shape on the drawn line. Cut some holes through the centers of the trees so the sky can peek through.

8. Remove the paper backing and, using the photomap as a guide with the web side down, position the silhouette of the trees, church roof, and cross over the bright sky, aligning them to suit your taste. Fuse the shape in place.

embellishing

Look at your quilt picture from a distance and note any areas you would like to improve. You can embellish your quilt top as desired with paint or extra tulle.

1. If desired, use a sponge to dab on some blue-gray fabric paint to soften the edges of the dark clouds. Use just a light hand; it's easy to add more if desired, but you can't remove it if you've used too much. You can also cut fabric shapes and use them to shape some of the clouds.

2. I cut strips of yellow tulle about 4" x 25" and folded them in half lengthwise to make a double thickness. I laid the strips over the sky to create rays of light. Then I used the cross as the center, with the rays radiating out from there. (I basted the layers together and then added the yellow tulle before basting the black tulle in place.)

finishing

For detailed instructions, refer to "Finishing Techniques" on page 45.

1. Layer the fused fabric picture with batting and backing; baste the layers together. Place the tulle on top and baste in place.

2. Machine quilt as desired. I quilted feathers radiating out from the cross over the yellow tulle rays of light and quilted meandering lines in the rest of the sky.

3. Mark a cutting line around the outside edges to straighten the sides and square up the corners. To prevent the outside edges from stretching, attach the binding before you trim the excess fabric.

4. Use the 2¼"-wide black strips to bind the edges.

5. Add a hanging sleeve using the same fabric as the backing.

6. Attach a signature label to your work of art.

FINISHING TECHNIQUES

Quilts consist of three layers: the quilt picture, or top, the backing, and the batting. For this method, I've added a fourth layer: tulle. Now that your quilt picture is done, you're ready to move on to the finishing stages.

backing fabrics

The quilt backing can be a fabric that continues the theme of the quilt. Keep in mind that bold prints might show through the light areas of your quilt picture, such as the sky. For the projects in this book, I've listed an adequate amount of backing fabric to have some leftover fabric to cut a hanging sleeve.

batting choices

I recommend a low-loft batting because each project will be a wall hanging. My preference is 100%-cotton batting that has a scrim, or thin mesh, that the fibers are woven through. A scrim helps stabilize the batting so it doesn't stretch out of shape easily, but it can make the batting difficult to hand quilt. Plan for at least 2" of extra batting around all edges of the quilt top.

layering the quilt

Before you layer the quilt picture, press your backing fabric. You may hand baste, pin baste, or spray baste the first three layers of the quilt. However, the fourth layer of tulle must be pinned or hand basted over the picture.

My preferred method is to use a temporary basting spray to put the first three layers together. If your quilt is large, you may want to get someone to help you.

1. Spread the backing, wrong side up, on a flat, clean surface. Anchor the corners with masking tape, taking care not to stretch the backing out of shape.

2. Cover any exposed area around the backing with paper to protect from overspray.

3. Center the batting over the backing, smoothing out any wrinkles.

4. Center the quilt picture, right side up, over the batting, smoothing out any wrinkles.

5. Carefully fold back half of the quilt picture; spray the batting. Lay the quilt picture back down and gently pat the surface. Repeat with the other half of the quilt picture.

6. Now fold back half of the picture *and* batting (they are now stuck together); spray the backing. Lay the batting and picture back down. Repeat to spray the other half of the backing.

tulle layer

You can add a variety of embellishments to your quilt under the tulle layer. This is the point where you need to include them, before you baste the tulle and start to quilt. For example, in "Deep Blue Sea" on page 23, I decided to randomly place some polyester stuffing over my clouds, under the tulle layer. "Coastal Garden" on page 31 has organza that has been cut into cloud shapes, which I laid over the clouds before adding the tulle.

Note: The tulle layer cannot be spray basted.

Carefully lay the tulle over the quilt picture. Pin along one edge all the way across the picture; then smooth out any wrinkles and pin another row about 6" away. Continue in this manner across the whole top. Tulle is kind of crawly, so pin it thoroughly. You may use small, curved safety pins or straight quilting pins. I use long, thin quilting pins. As you pin, bury the point of the pin in the batting. I usually make the pin go in and out, in and out, and then in again to embed the point in the batting. This will help keep those points from sticking you as you work, and it also makes them less likely to snag the tulle during the quilting process. When quilting, you will remove the pins as you come to them.

Note: If an accident happens and you stick yourself, move away from the quilt. You don't want to have to remove a spot of blood from your work of art. After you are all better, you can start again.

loose threads

Some people worry about the loose threads that appear on the edges of the cut pieces. This is how I recommend handling them.

1. Before adding the tulle layer, remove the most obvious threads.

2. Ignore the threads during the quilting process.

3. When quilting is complete, deal with only the threads that bother you. They can usually be picked up with your fingernails, through the tulle holes. A pair of tweezers comes in handy for tough ones.

I feel that the threads help create a watercolor, or blended, effect in the quilt picture. So, I only worry about the ones that offend my eye.

quilting

You'll need to quilt your basted project by machine, with lines that are close enough together to stitch over each square. Choose threads that enhance the picture. If you don't want the threads to show, use invisible, monofilament thread. I have used cotton, rayon, and invisible threads. Use what you like and can handle easily. I recommend using the same color in the bobbin as you do on the

top. As you stitch, hold the quilt sandwich loosely with your hands on either side of the needle. Sometimes the tulle layer will start to slide along with the direction of the sewing, but you can prevent that with your hand guidance.

Hint: Keep a practice "sample" sandwich near your machine to test thread tension.

If you're a beginning quilter or you're not comfortable with free-motion quilting, you may want to sew straight or wavy (almost straight) lines all over the quilt. Use a walking foot for straight or wavy quilting lines.

You may choose to try one of the following stitch designs.

*   Sew horizontal lines through each row of squares.

*   Sew diagonal lines in one direction through the squares.

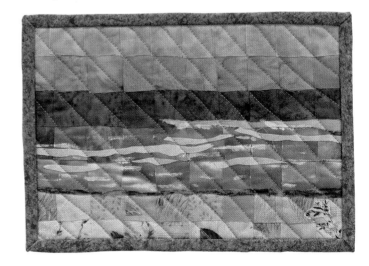

- Sew diagonal lines in both directions for a diamond grid.

Remember to stitch a quilting line over each square of fabric. The fabric squares are held in place only by the fusible foundation, and if not stitched, they might come loose over time.

If you have some experience with free-motion quilting or want to try it, your stitching can be as fancy as you desire. Use a darning foot for free-motion quilting.

Here is a close-up of the water in "Pacific Beach."

You'll want to keep an even amount of stitching over the whole surface of the quilt. This prevents one part from drawing up more than another. As mentioned above, it's important to quilt over each fabric square. For a nice effect, create designs that enhance the picture, such as swirls in the waves, leaves on floral areas, and stippling in the clouds. Use your imagination and have fun.

The last option is to take your quilt to a professional for quilting. If you do so, be sure to take along this book so that the quilter will understand the tulle overlay. Just take the four layers without basting them first.

Squaring up the quilt picture

When you complete the quilting, you may need to square up and flatten, or block, your quilt picture. I've included two methods for flattening your quilt.

1. Turn it over and lightly steam iron the quilt from the back. Lay it flat to dry.

2. Completely wet it. Fill your washer with cold water, dip the quilt in the washer to saturate it, and hand squeeze it. Skip to the spin cycle and spin it to remove most of the water. Stand there during the process and stop the action when the spin cycle is done. Do not let the agitator work. Take the quilt out of the washer and lay it on a clean, flat surface. Tug on the corners of your quilt to get the shape you want, and then let it dry. The drying takes some time, but this works very well.

After the quilt is dry, use a large square ruler to draw a line along the top edge to mark the top two corners. Measure down from the top line, through the quilt center, to mark the bottom edge. Then, using that same dimension, measure down from each top corner to mark the bottom corners. Measure the width between the corners at the bottom and the top to make sure they are the same distance apart. Draw a line along the bottom and along each side edge. Use a walking foot to stitch a line around the perimeter, just inside the drawn line. I prefer to wait to trim the extra batting and backing away until after I've attached binding. This prevents the edges from stretching as you sew.

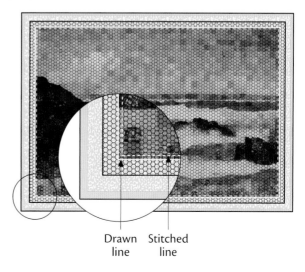

Drawn line   Stitched line

binding

I like to choose a binding fabric that will frame my picture. Sometimes I use plain black. Sometimes I pick a fabric that looks like wood so that my picture will look more "framed." Other times I choose a color in the picture that I want to emphasize. You can take your quilted picture to the fabric shop and hold it up against many fabrics until you find just the right one.

I prefer a double-fold binding made from strips cut on the straight grain (as opposed to bias-cut strips). I used 2¼"-wide strips for the projects in this book. You will cut enough strips to go around the perimeter of your quilt plus about 10" extra for making seams and turning corners.

1. To make one long, continuous strip, place the strips right sides together at right angles and stitch diagonally across the corner as shown. Trim the excess fabric, leaving a ¼"-wide seam allowance, and press the seam allowance open.

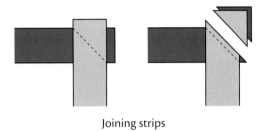

Joining strips

2. Press the strip in half lengthwise, with wrong sides together and raw edges aligned.

3. Unfold the binding at one end and turn under the beginning edge at a 45° angle as shown. Unfold the beginning edge and trim ¼" beyond the fold. Refold the edge, leaving a ¼"-wide edge turned under.

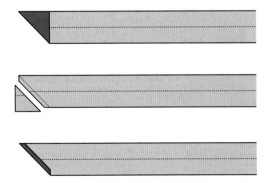

4. Refold the strip lengthwise, wrong sides together; then, beginning with the angled end of the binding strip, align the raw edge of the strip along the marked line on the quilt top. Starting in about the middle of the right side (not at a corner) and beginning 3" from the strip's angled end, use a walking foot and a ¼"-wide seam allowance to stitch the binding strip to the quilt. Stop ¼" from the first corner and backstitch.

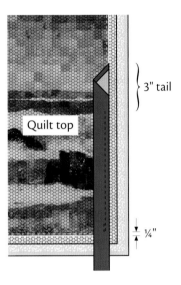

5. Remove the quilt from the sewing machine. Turn the quilt so that you will be stitching down the next side. Fold the binding up and away from the quilt; the fold will form a 45° angle. Fold the binding back down again, even with the edge of the sewn binding, align the raw edge of the binding with the marked line, and pin as shown. Begin with a backstitch at the fold of the binding and continue stitching along the edge of the quilt top, mitering each corner as you come to it.

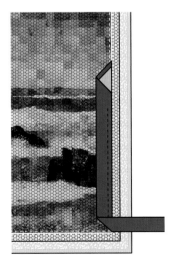
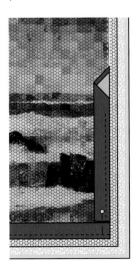

6. When you near the beginning of the binding strip, stop 3" before you reach it and backstitch. Remove the quilt from the machine. Trim the binding tail 1" longer than needed and tuck the end inside the beginning of the strip. Pin it in place, making sure the strip lies flat. Stitch the rest of the binding.

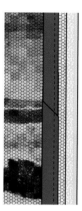

7. Carefully trim the extra backing and batting even with the raw edge of the binding. Turn the binding to the back of the quilt. Using thread to match the binding, hand stitch the binding in place so that the folded edge covers the row of machine stitching. At each corner, fold the binding to form a miter on the back of the quilt.

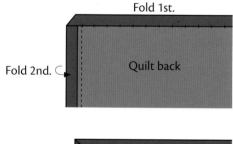

Fold 1st.

Fold 2nd.

Quilt back

hanging sleeve

To hang your quilt for display, you'll need to attach a hanging sleeve or rod pocket to the back of the quilt.

1. Cut an 8½"-wide piece of fabric to a length equal to the width of your quilt plus 1". This will yield a 4"-wide finished sleeve.

2. To hem the short ends, fold under ½" at each end, and then fold under ½" again. Press and stitch the folds in place. This is a nice place to use some of your fancy stitches if you wish.

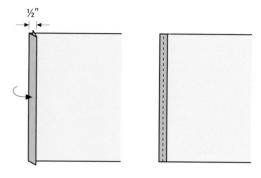

½"

3. With wrong sides together, sew the raw edges together, using a ¼"-wide seam allowance. Press the seam allowance open.

4. Position the sleeve so that the seam is centered along the underside, next to the quilt back.

5. Pin the sleeve to the back of the quilt, just below the bound edge. Whipstitch both the top and bottom of the sleeve to the quilt, being careful that your stitches don't go through to the front of the quilt. Stitch the back of each tube end to the quilt.

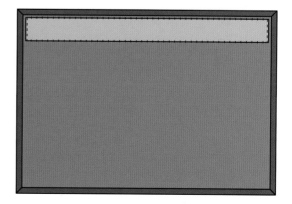

signature label

It's not finished yet. There are many ways to sign your quilt. The most important thing is that you *sign* it. Many of us have quilts that were made years ago. Most of these quilts were not signed, so they raise questions: Who actually made this? When was it made? Was there a special reason the person made it?

On my early quilts, I used a permanent marker and simply signed and dated the quilt on the back, near the binding. Now I like to do more.

- You can purchase cute labels to sign, date, and stitch onto the back of your quilt.

- Some people who like to hand stitch enjoy embroidering their information.

- You can make a little block using fabrics from the front.

- Appliqué a shape with your details on it.

- I often make a block on my computer containing all the pertinent information and print it on pretreated paper-backed fabric. I then remove the paper, turn under the edges, and hand stitch it onto the quilt. You can include pictures, borders, and whatever else your heart desires.

- If you put handwriting on your label, make sure to use a permanent pen intended for fabric.

No matter what type of label you choose, be sure to at least include your first and last name, the city and state where you live, and the date of completion. If you've used someone else's pattern, you should give credit on the label, noting the designer and the book or magazine you used. Optional additions include sentiments and verses (I like to include a Bible verse), and if the quilt is a gift, the occasion as well as the names of the recipient and giver.

If you enter your quilts in shows, you will usually be required to have a label with your complete address and phone number, so you might as well include that. When I am designing a label on my computer, I use large fonts for the important stuff and then smaller fonts for the details. A picture is nice too. Below are some examples of quilt labels.

displaying your quilt picture

To hang your quilt, you may slip your choice of hanging device through the sleeve and attach it to the wall. Here are some tips.

- Curtain rods are a nice way to hang a quilt. The quilts in this book are small enough that you shouldn't have a problem.

- Small quilts can be hung on a dowel.

- A piece of wood molding from the home-building center can also make a nice hanger. Have it cut about ½" shorter than the width of your quilt, and drill a hole close to each end for a nail or screw. Insert the molding into the quilt sleeve and mount the molding on the wall. Tug the quilt to cover the edges of the wood.

- There are many choices of quilt hangers available for purchase.

- Think about where you plan to hang your quilts. Remember that direct sunlight will damage the colors over time. You can minimize the damage by rotating your quilts frequently.

Quilts add a homey touch wherever you hang them. These art quilts are like paintings. Enjoy them.

cleaning and washing suggestions

Most of the time a wall hanging can just be shaken out to remove dust. If that is not enough, place a clean sock over the end of a vacuum cleaner hose and use medium suction to vacuum off the dust, or use a damp cloth to freshen the edges.

When it is necessary to wash your quilt, use a mild detergent. Fill the washer with tepid water and dissolve the detergent in the water. Submerge the quilt and let it soak for a few minutes. Stand by the washer to keep it from agitating. Gently agitate the quilt by hand and squeeze to wash out any dirt.

Move the dial to the spin cycle and let the washer spin out the water. Move the dial to the rinse cycle, let it fill with clean water, and then stop the action. Once again, swish and squeeze by hand. Then, move the dial to the spin cycle again and let the washer spin out the water. You might need to rinse twice to remove all the soap. Remove the quilt from the washer, and then pull and flatten it until you get the correct shape. (Use a ruler to make sure it's square.) Lay it flat to dry.

GALLERY

Among Giants, *43″ x 86″.*

What a lovely sunny day in the forest! I used tiny ½″ squares, free-cut shapes, and long strips that replicated the stringy bark of the redwood. The inspiration photo was taken in Richardson's Grove Park near Garberville, California, by Gary Durbin.

Whispers of Hope, *44" x 52".*

During Easter week the trees in our city exploded in blossoms. The delicate blossom area in this quilt is made entirely of thread, with crystals to enhance. The inspiration photo was taken by Gary Durbin.

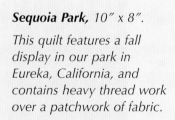

Sequoia Park, *10" x 8".*

This quilt features a fall display in our park in Eureka, California, and contains heavy thread work over a patchwork of fabric.

Looking Back, *38" x 53".*

Quilt front is shown above.
Quilt back is shown at right.

I discovered four pictures of my sister, Connie, and me. Dad had taken a back shot as well as front shots, and I just had to try a two-sided quilt. The back view of the girls is appliqué, and the front view is paint on white fabric. Connie, the taller, blonde girl, is the grandmother of the "Sunny Girls" on page 55.

Greg's Gone Fishing, 55" x 50".

This is a memory quilt for my long-time friend Jan, featuring her son. The inspiration photo of Greg fishing in a stream in the Colorado Rocky Mountains was taken by Kimberly Peticolas, Greg's sister.

Sunny Girls, 90" x 70".
23,100 squares, 1/2" x 1/2".

This quilt features Claire and Hannah, my sister's twin granddaughters. The inspiration photo was taken by Diane Lusty.

"DEEP BLUE SEA" PHOTOMAP (See page 23 for project instructions.)

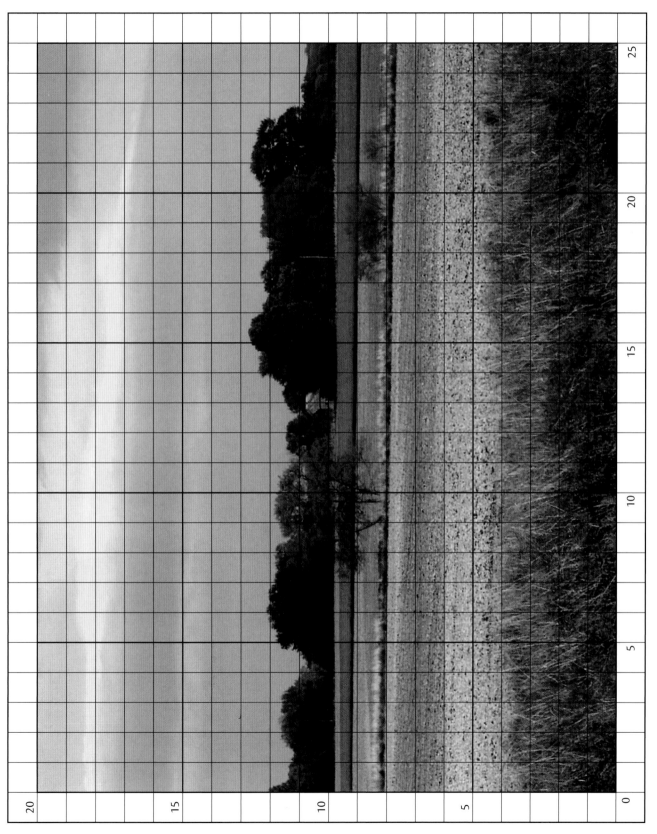

"A TIME TO SOW" PHOTOMAP (See page 27 for project instructions.)

"COASTAL GARDEN" PHOTOMAP (See page 31 for project instructions.)

"PACIFIC BEACH" PHOTOMAP (See page 37 for project instructions.)

"MORNING LIGHT" PHOTOMAP (See page 41 for project instructions.)

TRANSPARENCY FORMS

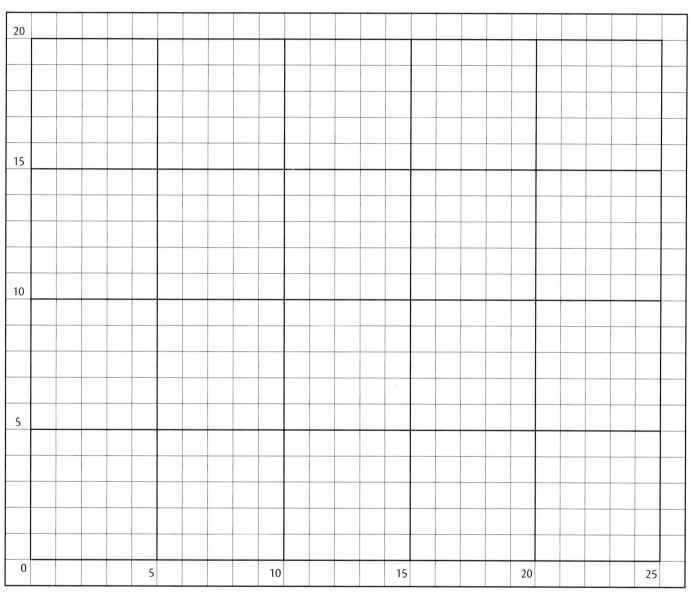

TRANSPARENCY FORM A

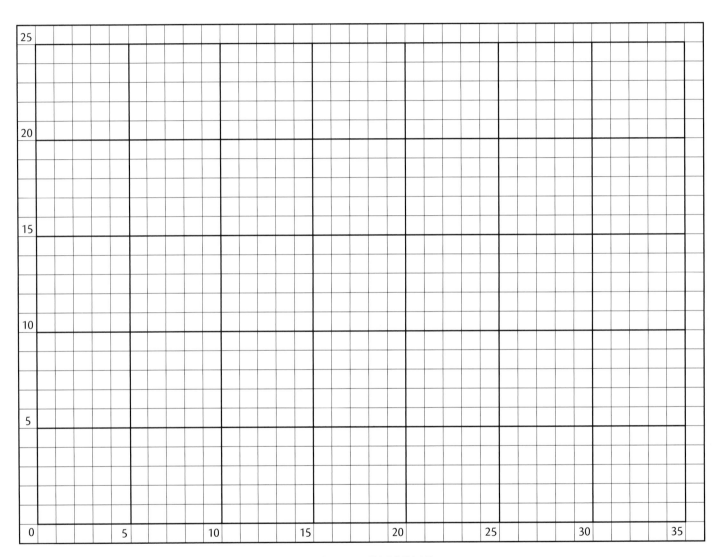

TRANSPARENCY FORM B

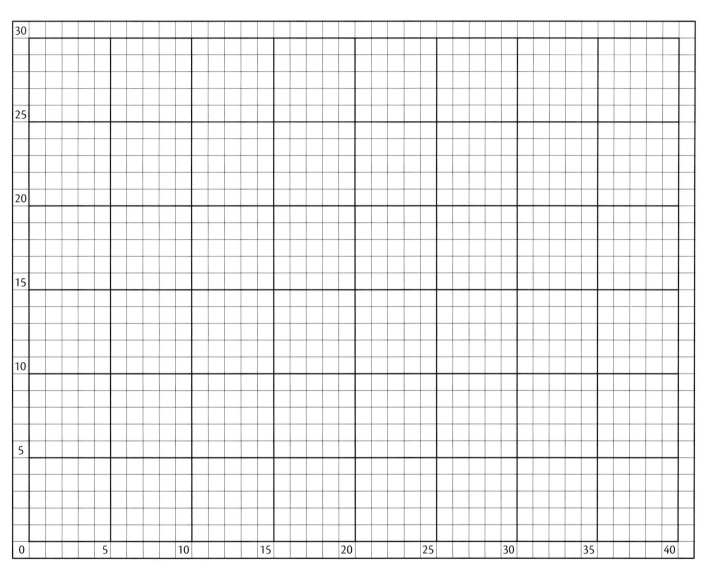

TRANSPARENCY FORM C

ABOUT THE AUTHOR

Pat Durbin is an award-winning quilter and a quilting teacher. She is a minister's wife who lives on the beautiful northern coast of California. Most of her years have been spent raising children and working in the church where her husband is the pastor. Her church work includes piano playing, choir directing, singing, teaching, and working in women's ministries. She also worked outside the home as a secretary and clerical worker for several years. Sewing clothing has always been a big part of her life, and this interest has expanded to include a passion for quilting. Pat has made many traditional quilts for family and friends.

Now, no longer working an outside job or raising children, she has more time to play. Recently her quilting has moved toward art quilts. She enjoys the freedom of style the quilt world today offers, where the artist within can thrive. Pat enjoys sharing quilting ideas, teaching, and developing friendships throughout the quilting community. She especially enjoys being a grandmother and passing on the talent of sewing and quilting to her lovely granddaughters, Christina and Amy, who live nearby and are now quilters developing styles of their own. So the art of quilting passes on to another generation.